A CITY IN FLAMES

A FIREWOMAN'S RECOLLECTIONS OF THE HULL BLITZ

by Esther Baker

assisted by Howard Baker

Hutton Press 1992

Published by the Hutton Press Ltd.,
130 Canada Drive, Cherry Burton,
Beverley, East Yorkshire HU17 7SB

Typeset and Printed by
Image Colourprint Ltd.,
Anlaby, Hull.

ISBN 1 872167 41 1

This book is dedicated to the memories of my husband Albert and my daughter Margaret.

CONTENTS

ASSISTANT'S NOTE

May 1991 marked the fiftieth anniversary of the severest raids of the Hull blitz, and the media coverage of that anniversary prompted my mother to recount to me some of her experiences during the war years. It struck me then as a story that should not be lost, and I therefore offered to help her record it. This book is the result.

Wherever possible I have checked my mother's recollections against the official record of events. In most cases the two match perfectly, in a few cases they are at variance. In these latter cases I have not amended her memories to match the record, for this is essentially a personal account based on perception at the time and recollection later. These may deceive but will always be more real to the individual than any objective record. I was once told by an old soldier that he never knew what he did on D-Day until he read the book years later, and that his version would have been very different. War, it seems, is like that.

On a personal note: I was born two years after the coming of peace, and it has been a revelation as well as a privilege to help set down this story from Hull's war. It is one person's view of the city's ordeal, but it reflects an overall spirit of courage, fortitude and good humour. On behalf of my generation, born after the last 'All Clear', I salute those who lived through those terrible days, and thank those who served in Hull's defence. But for you there would have been precious little city left for us to be born in.

Howard Baker

INTRODUCTION

I was born in Kingston upon Hull on 17th July 1913, and although I have visited other cities and other countries Hull has always remained my home. The very word 'home' implies comfort and safety, and certainly today I find reassurance in my life-long familiarity with the city. Yet for a period, some half a century ago, Hull became the setting for the most uncomfortable and frightening experiences of my life, for like many others I endured the Luftwaffe's attempts to destroy the city. I was also granted a 'grandstand view' of the proceedings, for during the period of the Blitz I served as a firewoman in the control room at the Central Fire Station, on Worship Street, and was married to one of the firemen engaged in the desperate struggle to save the city from destruction.

The facts of that struggle have been set down before, but facts are not feelings, and all who lived through those days felt emotions which would never be reflected in any official document, lived through experiences which would remain with them until their dying day, but which have gone largely unrecorded.

It is of such experiences that this book is made. Mine were not unique, and I am sure there are those who suffered greater hardship and terror during that time, saw sights and engaged in exploits which make mine seem comparatively modest. As a member of Hull's A.R.P. Service I was just a tiny part of a large team of men and women, all of whom worked tremendously hard and endured great perils to ensure that the Luftwaffe did not prevail. In telling this story I would not wish to give the impression that my contribution was any greater than that of anyone else during those times. My husband Albert and I did our jobs, just as others did. We did them no better than anyone else, and I hope that we did them no worse. I am just fortunate in having a son with the patience and the ability to help me set down my account of that period, as I remember it. All those who were dearest to me in those challenging years are now gone: my parents, sisters, husband and daughter. I am grateful to my son for enabling me to record their existence and preserve their memory.

The fear, sorrow, comradeship and excitement of those days are as real and vivid to me now as the flowers beyond my window at this moment, but in some cases the passage of fifty years has blurred the details of names, times and places. The reader may encounter imprecision, perhaps even discover inaccuracy, but I trust that I will be forgiven for these flaws. Even an imprecise account is better than no account at all, when the tale is worth the telling. And no vagueness of mine can detract from the heroism of Hull and its people during those grim and savage days.

Esther Baker.

CHAPTER ONE

FROM ONE WAR TO ANOTHER

Being born in 1913 I had my first experience of war at a very early age. Although shielded by incomprehension from the full horror of the Great War I can still recall the effect on the city when the buzzer sounded to warn of an impending Zeppelin raid. Such was the fear inspired by this sinister new form of warfare that my father, a foundry worker at C.D. Holmes, would herd my mother and his whole brood - five daughters and a son - all the way from our home on Tadman Street to St Nicholas Church Hall, close to Pickering Park, where we would sleep on the floor in the company of what seemed to be the entire population of Hessle Road.

That long trek to safety made the war an exhausting dream: an unreal phantasm of darkness and distant explosions, but I can recall seeing the devastation caused to Queen Street market, and remember the excitement of a night when the buzzer failed to give its warning, and looking from the window of my Aunt Sabrah's home at the corner of George's Terrace we saw a Zeppelin high overhead, trapped in a cone of searchlight beams, like a huge insect pinned to the sky by silver needles.

Apart from those fragmentary impressions, and a vague awareness of shortages, my most lasting memory of that conflict is of the celebrations which marked its conclusion. We lived in a terrace, and even though I was only five years old the 'terrace tea' which marked the Armistice made a great impression on me, with the adults dancing and singing, the houses draped in flags and one of our neighbours bringing his piano out into the terrace to give musical support to the proceedings.

With the excitement over I settled into a normal Hessle Road childhood. As always in youngster's recollections I remember that the sun shone most of the time, and invariably on August Bank Holiday Mondays when we would troop down to Corporation Pier, board the New Holland Ferry and pay a visit to Cleethorpes. Now, in an era when a continental holiday is available to most people, it is hard to believe that a single day's outing was our only holiday, but then those were hard times for most people. Bread was never bought in our home, I remember, instead my mother would bake it herself, and when the stove was full to capacity she would send us off with the remaining tins of dough in a pram to Cheethams Bakery, where they would bake it for us. I remember, too, waiting for the tram on Monday mornings and seeing the women queuing outside the pawn shop on Neptune Street, waiting to pawn their husband's best suits; retrieving them on the following Friday. My Aunt Sabrah supplemented her household income by taking in the fisher girls who came down from Scotland each year. All wore knitted shawls and clogs, and seemed to live on a diet of a strange soup called 'Auchtermaucherty' a pot of which they always had simmering on her stove; or simmering as much as anything can that is nearly solid with barley and carrots.

Every Sunday morning my father would take us for a walk to the Saspirella Shop on Hessle Road - perhaps it had a real name but that's how we knew it - and after being treated to lemonade and sweets we would walk with him to Bank End and on to Riverside Quay, where we would wave to the sailors working on the decks of the towering ships. I could never have imagined then that one day those grey waters would glow with reflected fire, like a lake of liquid gold, as the vast quay blazed from end to end and stained they sky crimson with its flames.

(left). A 17 year old with a first boyfriend. Every seaside town at her feet and not a care in the world.

(below). Albert with the Ariel.

Hessle Road life was hard, yes, but a fairly simple affair and largely uneventful. Even so, my childhood does hold one memorable dramatic incident. I recall playing in Tadman Street in the warmth of a summer day in 1921, and how the people around me paused on the pavement to stare up as a huge airship floated overhead, heading towards the Humber. And I remember how, when the airship had passed from sight, the silence of that August afternoon was suddenly rent by a thunderous explosion that froze people where they stood and brought others dashing from their homes to be greeted by shocked cries of "Its crashed! It's crashed!"

The movement of people that followed was spontaneous and universal; children and adults set off towards Corporation Pier at a gallop. My sister Anne was among them; on her bike and away like a lamplighter. I was already pelting after her when my mother grabbed me, thereby denying me the chance to become one of history's spectators. I had to wait until Anne returned to learn of the shattered wreck now lying out in the Humber; a wreck which had once been the airship R-38, and which had taken 44 men to their graves.

At the age of 14 I left Daltry Street School and began work at George Winn's Bakery on Dagger Lane. The working day began at 6 a.m., and I can remember taking the tram to Osborne Street, walking over Monument Bridge and down Prince's Dock Side in the early morning gloom. In those days, of course, Queen's Gardens was still Queen's Dock, and Monument Bridge would open periodically to allow barges to pass through. As the city's bridges do to this day, it provided an ideal excuse for lateness!

Not that I ever wanted to be late. Winn's was a wonderful bakery that was well-known for its delicious bread, and also for its lovely cakes and buns. The bakery had a shop on Prospect Street called David Little's, and their window was always full of the gorgeous things we made, like pineapple creams and battenburgs and chocolate eclairs. At Christmas we'd do a nativity scene, with figures made of marzipan and fondant and shiny sponge sugar, and at Easter we'd create a huge chocolate Easter egg to stand open in the window, with chocolates displayed inside. We made the chocolates too, at Winns, and Brandy Snap for Hull Fair and cabin biscuits for ships. These latter were a lovely light brown when they came out of the ovens, and they were packed and sent off to sea in huge whicker containers like laundry baskets.

Unfortunately Winns closed after two years, but by then I'd learnt a lot about the trade, and at 16 I went to work at William Jacksons's bakery on Victoria Street. It was there, within six months, that I met my husband-to-be, Albert.

Albert was handsome young man and an expert sugar boiler; skilled in creating all manner of sweets, from toffees to mint rock. To add to the attraction he possessed a motorbike - an Ariel 250 - and it wasn't long before we were flying along the roads together, visiting seaside resorts from Bridlington to Blackpool - quite an eye-opener for a girl who'd only ever been as far as Cleethorpes. Eventually - after the Ariel was replaced by an OK Supreme - we graduated to the Lake District, Wales and Scotland; journeys which drew reproof from my mother.

"Why don't you have the kind of holiday where you take a suitcase, like normal people?" I can remember her chiding me. "Instead of racing round the country with a haversack on your back."

It was a way of life that suited us, though, and a

simple and inexpensive way to leave behind the cares of the Thirties. We were aware of the arrival of the Depression, though not seriously affected by it, but of wider world events we took little notice. Young people are not inclined to acknowledge much outside themselves, and when eventually we married, in August 1938, we were unaware that we were taking our decision in the shadow of far more momentous events.

Our first home was a little house on Ledbury Road, off Priory Road, and for exactly a year we lived a happy, uncomplicated life there. Yet as the superb summer of 1939 began to fade even we became aware of the drift to war. When friends in the Territorial Army are mobilised, and Anderson Shelters begin appearing in people's gardens, even the most determinedly idyllic of people have to acknowledge that all is not as it should be. Yet still it came as a shock to hear Neville Chamberlain's voice on that fateful day, delivering not so much a declaration of war as a declaration of utmost sorrow.

Albert missed the speech - a friend had begged a trip on his motorbike in order to visit her Territorial boyfriend, who had been sent to a camp on the coast. But I was not alone; Ledbury Road, like the country as a whole, had been awaiting the announcement, and people kept dropping in to discuss the news, then passing on to other houses. The street was in motion; a motion powered by excitement and apprehension. Within hours it seemed the latter was justified; as evening fell the chilling wail of the sirens sounded across the city and friends rushed from across the street to invite me into their shelter - at that point we were without one. In fact I'd have been better off unprotected; their shelter was badly finished off and a jagged edge of corrugated iron carved an agonising gouge from my leg - and after all that it was a false alarm!

Eventually the sounding of the all-clear relieved the tension, but we scrambled out into a world that had changed irrevocably. The morning news proved that beyond doubt, informing us that the liner *Athenia*, carrying evacuee children to America, had been torpedoed and sunk, with terrible loss of life. I remember sitting in a neighbour's home and feeling cold with horror as the announcer delivered this news. It was impossible to understand how such savagery had come among us, and frightening to have no idea at all of what the future would bring.

Albert and I on our wedding day, August 1938

CHAPTER TWO

EARLY DAYS AND FIRST RAIDS

What the immediate future brought, of course, was a succession of calamities starting with the invasion of Norway and ending with the evacuation from Dunkirk and the fall of France. On a personal level, however, we had a domestic disaster to contend with - Albert was made redundant. The introduction of rationing meant there was too little sugar available to keep a sugar boiler gainfully employed. Thus it came about that he applied and was accepted into the Auxiliary Fire Service; almost following in the footsteps of his father, who was a police sergeant. In those days Hull had a police fire brigade.

It cannot have been easy for the officers of the fire brigade to come to terms with this sudden influx of untrained Auxiliaries, and the Auxiliaries themselves had their share of problems - such as being issued with only a single uniform. Many times during his basic training Albert returned home icy cold and shivering, having spent the day wearing a tunic saturated during some exercise. It soon became clear, however, that regardless of such discomforts he was enjoying his new role. The men he was training alongside came from all walks of life, and were a good bunch. I remember the three Bills - Bill Spaven, Bill Hewitt and Bill Priestman - and Jim Wardby and George Lacey. Then there was Wilf Crowther, who'd been a watch repairer at Carmichaels, Charlie Frost, who was always a bit of a rebel, Ted Wells, who always stood ramrod straight like a guardsman, and Clifford Turner who was the youngest Auxiliary at Central and was destined to earn himself the George Medal in the first big fire of the blitz.

After his basic training Albert was initially sent to the Temple Street Depot, off Beverley Road, where those halcyon days of the Ariel and OK Supreme came in useful - he was detailed as a despatch rider, being sent out to guide in any convoys of reinforcements arriving from other regions. Sometimes he would get a break and come puttering round to Ledbury Road on his motorbike for a quick cup of tea, and then it was just like the old days. After a while, however, he was transferred to Central Fire Station at Worship Street, and detailed to firefighting duties.

In those day's Hull was unique in having 'The Venners', as they were known - a traffic signalling system controlled from Central Fire Station which over-rode the normal traffic lights, allowing the fire appliances unhindered passage through the city centre. Activation of the Venners was accompanied by the clamour of a bell, and whenever I was in town and heard that bell I would rush to a suitable point to watch the vehicles pass. Often I was rewarded with a glimpse of Albert at the wheel of one of the appliances - usually the emergency tender - and I would feel so very proud of him then.

For my own part I, like many other housewives, spent most of my time grappling with the domestic problems created by war - of which rationing was perhaps the most exasperating. I can remember trying to stretch 4 oz of butter, 4 oz of bacon and 2 oz of sugar over a week, and being unimpressed when some Minister or other told us that we were all getting healthier through not eating so much. Like most people I was not taken in by that stuff about carrots making you see in the dark, but years later I would find myself passing the same fib on to my children to get them to eat theirs! I can remember queueing for ages at Rosenberg's greengrocers, to emerge with just a single tomato. I can remember, too, trying to produce culinary masterpieces from concoctions such as powdered potato and dried eggs - the latter being

(above). Preparing for the worst...Auxiliaries learning to handle jets at William Wright Dock in October 1939. With only a single uniform each, Albert and his colleagues were frequently left saturated and freezing by these training sessions. Courtesy of Hull City Record Office.

Auxiliaries learning to handle one of the professional brigade's wheeled escapes during a training session at the C.W.S. Warehouse, Cumberland Street, in June 1940. Courtesy of Hull City Record Office.

(left). The city's peacetime fire stations were insufficient to cope with the demands of wartime, so a variety of buildings were pressed into service as makeshift fire stations. This Photograph, taken in 1939, shows fire fighters at a station established in the tram sheds on Hedon Road. The picture was loaned to us by Mrs Eve Hopper, whose brother Bob Johnson served with the AFS throughout the war.

(right). An AFS crew pictured outside the Little Theatre Fire Station, Kingston Square. Note the cat in the armsof the fireman at bottom right. As homes were destroyed stray cats became a familiar feature, and were often adopted as mascots. This picture was loaned by Mrs Vera Moffat, whose husband Robert is on the second rank up, fourth from the left.

13

The work-horse of the blitz... a trailer pump and crew pictured outside the Little Theatre Station, Kingston Square, in October 1939. There was a shortage of suitable Brigade vehicles so initially these machines were towed to incidents by any available vehicle, with taxi cabs frequently being used. The second fireman from the left is Mr Charles Kenningham, who became the mobilising officer in Central's control room.

Albert and other trainee firemen at the Brigade's training depot at Swanland in 1940. Albert is the second from the right on the second row up.

served up as omelettes that you could have soled your shoes with. And I can remember discovering that dried banana was repulsive - you added the water and it went all slithery. I recall that whalemeat was on offer at some butchers shops, but I didn't fancy the idea of eating whales. Funnily enough, though, one wartime item did prove a hit with Albert. He developed a taste for condensed milk in his tea, and stuck to it for years after rationing ended.

At some point our Anderson shelter arrived, but apart from the barrage balloons, the wailing sirens, the sandbagged buildings and the fact that my Aunt Sabrah taught her budgie to squeak 'Don't forget your gas mask, Bill', the war didn't really impinge on me. I would hear the anti-aircraft guns in the distance, and Albert would tell me of incendiary raids he'd been turned out to, but somehow the war seemed strangely unreal at the time. For me it didn't really arrive until midsummer.

On the afternoon of July 1st 1940 I played tennis with a girlfriend at a court on Priory Road. Shortly after five-o'-clock we heard the thrum of engines overhead, but since it seemed to be a lone aircraft and no sirens had sounded, we barely gave it a thought. Soon afterwards, however, there came the sound of anti-aircraft fire, and a series of distant explosions. Then, far across on the other side of the city, a column of thick, black smoke rose up on the horizon. Albert was on duty that day and as I watched the oily stain spread across the sky I felt, for the first time, the onset of anxiety; realising that he would probably be turned out from Central to attend the incident, which looked very big and nasty. Had I realised exactly what was beneath that column of smoke I would have been petrified rather than anxious.

The lone raider had dropped several bombs around the Saltend oil terminal, and fragments from one of these ripped through a tank containing thousands of gallons of petrol. The petrol caught fire as it spewed out of the holes, and was threatening to ignite the main bulk still inside the tank. It was also flowing in a blazing stream towards the surrounding tanks. Such was the sight that awaited the crews when they arrived at the scene. As Albert freely admitted later, he had never seen a fire so enormous and evil-looking since he joined, and had never been so scared in all his life.

What followed was a desperate struggle to save not only the tank but the whole terminal and possibly a good part of the city, for if the fire had spread unchecked it could have produced an explosion of awesome proportions. In order to prevent this it was necessary for the firefighters to drain the damaged tank of its remaining petrol while pouring foam onto that which was burning and at the same time playing jets on the surrounding tanks to keep them cool. By the end of that night the situation had been brought under control and five George Medals had been earned; one by Clifford Turner, one by a professional fireman called Jack Owen and three others by Saltend staff.

Albert returned from the scene next day, exhausted, bedraggled and stinking with smoke, oil and foul-smelling foam, having spent most of the night perched high on one of the tanks, amidst the billowing smoke, playing a jet on the surrounding tanks. He seemed to have aged ten years overnight, but that was hardly surprising in the circumstances. I suppose I realised then that being a fireman was not simply about sitting behind the wheel of a shiny fire appliance; it was also about standing on top of a huge tank of petrol with flames licking around it. From

*One of Albert's early major incidents; Saner & Harrison's warehouse.
Squeezed between the river and the narrow confines of High Street it was a
very awkward job for the firefighters. Courtesy of Hull City Record Office.*

then on I took more notice of his work, and became more aware of the problems that he and the others were having to overcome.

The Saltend oil installation was a legitimate target, I suppose, but the raids that followed seemed to be indiscriminate. with people's homes suffering most. I remember a bomb causing a lot of destruction in Morrill Street, and another one wrecking many houses in Strathmore Avenue. Albert and his colleagues frequently worked alongside the wardens and rescue squads at such incidents, with everyone struggling to extricate those trapped in the wreckage while themselves often imperilled by everything from falling masonry to leaking gas.

In peacetime, of course, incoming firemen were given a lot of training before they became operational, and even then they would only occasionally encounter a really big incident. Albert and his colleagues had the worst of both worlds; hurried training and a regular supply of major incidents! As conscientious in this job as he had been at Jacksons, Albert took copious notes during the theory lectures, practiced things like knots and lines endlessly and tried hard to learn from each fire he attended. But in those early days every fire seemed to face his crew with problems that they had not encountered before, and the Luftwaffe did not help by bringing in new variations such as the explosive incendiary, the landmine that came down by parachute, and eventually the butterfly bomb.

The explosive incendiaries started to come down towards the end of 1940, and on one night alone they set fire to nearly fifty buildings across the city, including one on Alfred Gelder Street which for a while threatened the Guildhall. Albert attended that one, and the new problem on that occasion was the bitter cold which froze the hoses and made the street like glass so that firemen skidded and flailed and fell as they fought the fire, pushed across the ice by the back-pressure from the jets.

Then on Christmas Eve he was one of over a hundred firemen who fought the massive blaze which destroyed Saner & Harrison's grain warehouse in High Street - and that time it was High Street itself which posed the new problem. When he returned from that one Albert remarked that in a way it was a more frightening setting than the Saltend tank had been, for it was claustrophobic and awkward. High Street was so narrow that there was no room to manoeuvre the pumps, no escape from the heat and glare, and no way to run clear as the floors collapsed and sent clouds of sparks and burning embers cascading onto the cobbles below.

Nevertheless Albert and the other Auxiliaries were learning - if only the hard way - which was just as well because the tempo of the raids was definitely increasing. As a result of this the Fire Brigade authorities now decreed that all firemen must reside within their Divisions, as close as possible to their fire stations. Since Albert was stationed at Central, we packed our bits and pieces, bade a rather sad farewell to Ledbury Road and our first married home, and moved into No. 10 New George Street, close to the city centre.

No 10 was a two-storey building, and ours was the upper flat. It was comfortable and quite spacious, but most important it was just a few seconds sprinting time from Central. In the months to come that sprint was to become a nightly ritual, and undertaken in the total darkness of the blackout it was also quite an adventure.

CHAPTER THREE

JOINING THE STRUGGLE

The flat in New George Street cost us eight shillings a week, and in addition to the normal fixtures and fittings it came complete with a bell which was operated from the control room at Central. A single ring meant that there was a fire, a double ring was the signal for an impending air raid. Either one prompted the ritual sprint, with Albert hurtling down the stairs and racing to Central to catch his appliance before it roared out of its bay. In all the time we were there he never missed a turn-out, although early on in the proceedings I almost sabotaged his efforts.

Like most people in those days I used a bicycle to get around the city, and returning home from a visit to my mother's one evening in January 1941 I thoughtlessly left it parked in the hallway at the bottom of the stairs. At some time during the night our bell clanged into life, and as I lay, sleep-blurred, hearing Albert clatter down the stairs, I remembered what I had done and realised with horror that catastrophe was inevitable. It was indeed, and not long in the coming - in the darkened hallway Albert ran full tilt into the waiting obstruction and went down in a flailing, jangling tangle. Fortunately he had time only to pick himself up blasphemously and unleash the bellowed accusation: "Which bloody idiot left this bike here!". He didn't have time to wait for the answer, which was just as well since I was now under the blankets and not inclined to own up. The matter was forgotten by the time he returned, but I never did it again.

March brought heavy raids, with about a hundred dead. Fountain Road was wrecked, and George Street suffered. I think this was when Redbourne Street and Westcott Street were devastated, and more than twenty people killed in Grindell Street. Or that might have been later. Despite such horrors people carried on, and even managed to enjoy themselves in small ways - I suppose the war added that dark contrast that makes small pleasures precious. The radio was one of these, for me. I listened to Churchill's speech in which he praised 'The Few', and I recall Alvar Liddel identifying himself before reading the news, so we didn't get taken in by imitations, I suppose. And I remember Worker's Playtime and shows like Garrison Theatre and Much Binding in the Marsh, and of course ITMA, with Tommy Handley. It was funny the way the catchphrases caught on like wildfire, so everywhere you'd hear people saying things like "Don't forget the diver", Can I do yer now, sir?" and "Mind my bike" - which certainly struck a chord with me! Then there was the funniest show of all - Lord Haw-Haw. We used to tune in to him without fail, for the fun of listening to him talk rubbish. I have to feel that the Germans couldn't have grasped the British sense of humour or they'd never have allowed him near a microphone.

We also went to the cinema quite frequently, to see stars like Charles Laughton, Basil Rathbone, Tyrone Power and Greer Garson. Sometimes the programme would be interrupted by the notice which flashed onto the screen to tell us that an air raid was in progress and that those who wished to leave should do so. Some people in the audience did, some didn't, and someone always came out with the line about 'If it's got your name on it...'. Albert and I always stayed, really because after taking the trouble to come we just didn't feel like leaving.

Another of our small pleasures was dancing, and when Albert was off duty we used to trip the light fantastic at places such as the Fulford, on Beverley Road, at the Beverley Road Baths and the dance hall

The end of Hammonds, and of many a happy evening's dancing. The wreckage
of the rooftop dance hall can be seen at the top of the building.
Courtesy of Hull City Rcord Office.

which in those days graced the top floor of Hammonds department store. It must be admitted that I didn't necessarily reserve such outings for Albert - when he was on duty I would sometimes team up with one or more of my sisters, and we'd take the floor with servicemen from many parts of the world, intrigued by their unfamiliar uniforms and strange accents. The Poles, I remember, were particularly charming and handsome, the Canadians rather quiet, the Australians tall and tanned. It is one of the latter that I particularly remember; a handsome young man called Dave, one of a pair of pilots with whom my sister Mabel and I danced at Beverley Road Baths one night. A week later Mabel and I were there again, but only one of them arrived - Dave had been lost over Germany. That first night he had given me his uniform patch as a souvenir, but the significance of it had not struck me at the time. It bore the insignia of a pathfinder squadron based across in Lincolnshire. The casualty rate among the pathfinders was high.

Soon afterwards tragedy came even closer to home when the first of Albert's colleagues were killed while on duty. It was the night of March 1st, 1941, and the biggest raid that we had seen so far. I remember that the two rings summoned him from the flat quite early in the evening, and shortly afterwards came the drone of the bombers, interspersed with startling bangs from the anti-aircraft guns. I stayed in the flat for quite a while, watching from the window as the searchlights probed the sky, and following the sequence of the raid; first the flares blossoming high over the city and bathing everything in a strange, white light, then the incendiaries cascading from the sky and clattering down on roof and street before bursting into gouts of fire. And finally the high explosives arrived with a whistling scream that terminated in a variety of ways,

depending on the distance; sometimes a distant muffled 'THUD!', sometimes a closer roar, and a couple of times a thunderous crash that shook the whole building. Eventually, after one of the latter, I abandoned my sightseeing, left the flat and did the sprint myself - running along Caroline Street, onto Worship Street and into the yard of Central Fire Station, where a substantial shelter had been built.

Substantial it might have been, but still the vibration of the bombs could clearly be felt inside, and as I and the other fire brigade wives huddled under the flickering bulbs we could hear the sounds of Central operating at full stretch - the shouted orders, the clamour of the station bells going down again and again, the crash of the huge wooden bay doors and the roar of the appliances as they surged out into Worship Street and raced away, bells pealing, into the chaotic night.

As the hours wore on we picked up snippets of information from new arrivals and officers who called in to check on us; each of them entering in a haze of dust and a stink of smoke that described the situation outside far more eloquently than words. The number of incidents was heading towards the hundred mark, with many of the fires reaching major proportions. There appeared to be no focus to the raid; bombs were being scattered across the city, and factories, schools, churches and homes alike were being blasted apart or engulfed by fire. A rumour came that an appliance had been buried by a collapsing building, and I sat in terror, thinking of Albert, until the news arrived that the crew was safe. The relief was short-lived, however, for soon there came word that several firemen had been killed at an incident close by, somewhere near North Bridge. The information was vague, the estimates of the dead varied, but it was

(left). A despatch rider leads an 'NFS day' parade of the Fire Brigade's peacetime 'red engines' through Victoria Square, during 'War Weapons Week' in February 1942. Courtesy Hull City Record Office.

(right). Behind the 'red engines' came the hastily manufactured wartime appliances.They were strictly utilitarian – ungainly in appearance and painted in battleship grey – but they served us well. Courtesy Hull City Record Office.

clear that something tragic had occurred - and the fear returned once more.

Only the dawn dispelled it, for it was then, as we emerged into a cold, grey world of smoke and blowing brick-dust, that we learned the truth. A bomb had landed beside a crew as they pitched a ladder to the upper window of a burning warehouse, and the blast had killed three firemen instantly. As I realised that it was not Albert's crew I was torn between overwhelming relief and sorrow for the agony of those wives who had lost their men. There was sorrow for the Brigade too; it was a closely knit community and to lose three men was a terrible blow.

I think it was then, as I walked home along the littered street, that I realised I could no longer be simply a spectator, but had to make some contribution to the desperate struggle that was going on around me. By the time I reached the flat I had decided to join the Fire Brigade.

I told Albert of my decision when eventually he came off duty. He was grimy and grey with fatigue, his uniform wet and filthy, his hands frozen and raw from the icy water splashing back from the jet he'd been manning for hours. As well as being exhausted he was upset by the loss of the men at North Bridge; feeling that their deaths could have been avoided had there been a firewatcher present to give access to the warehouse without the need for a ladder. Every building was supposed to have its complement of firewatchers, but sometimes they were missing - in this case with tragic results.

Albert accepted my decision with surprisingly little protest; previously he had been rigidly traditional about a wife's place being in the home, but that was in peacetime. Now even he had come to accept that it was a case of 'all hands to the pumps'.

The following week I put in my application, and even as it was being processed I received - as if in retaliation for my presumption - my own personal piece of the blitz.

It was delivered as part of a fairly heavy raid during which several bombs fell in the vicinity of Central, but all the same it took me completely by surprise because No. 10 appeared intact as I approached it after leaving the shelter. Even when damage became visible it seemed slight at first - the front door had been ripped off and all the windows blown in, but that would have been little more than an inconvenience by current standards. But additionally a bomb - perhaps the same one - had struck an oil installation at the end of the street - Thelwells, I think it was - and oil from a pierced tank had run blazing down the gutters of New George Street, churning out oily black smoke that had then poured into the house through the gaping windows and doorway. The effect was astounding; unlike anything I had seen before or have witnessed since. Our flat now resembled the inside of a chimney. Every inch of the interior was coated with a fur of thick, greasy black soot, as if the whole place had been carpeted, decorated and furnished in matching black velvet. The effect was so complete, so total, that I could not properly distinguish a feature of the room, or even define the positions of the furniture; the place had been transformed into a great big box of total blackness.

I was so shocked by the sight that I burst into tears on the spot, then wandered in a daze down the street, where I bumped into Mrs Northgrave, who had a house on Caroline Street and billeted several firemen. She took me back to her home and gave me the standard cure for a crisis; a good cup of tea. After a while I was joined by my sisters Mabel and Anne, who had come in from the outskirts of the city to see that I was alright. Together we returned and surveyed the scene, but it was obvious that nobody could live in such conditions and accordingly I moved in to share Mabel's house on Bristol Road, while Albert was billeted in the New Manchester Hotel on George Street, in the company of several other firemen who had lost their homes. It was hardly an arrangement suited to a young married couple, but at least we were in the same city at a time when so many husbands and wives were separated by thousands of miles, and sometimes I was able to visit him at the hotel. In the meantime an AFS man who was a painter and decorator by trade was detailed to make our flat habitable once more, and this he did in about three weeks.

There were further raids during that period and as the sirens wailed Mabel and I would grab a pillow and blankets and retire to her shelter to sleep. Sometimes we would be invited into the shelter of her neighbours, Betty and Tom Rose and would stay up half the night playing cards. It was nice to have company but unfortunately Tom smoked a pipe which he appeared to load with 'flag-edge flake' - a term used by my mother for any foul-smelling tobacco - and the atmosphere in the enclosed space of their Anderson soon became pretty awful. I think it was the only occasion during the entire war when I actually felt that my gas mask might offer some benefit.

Actually there was one other occasion, and it fell during this same period. Mabel and I had gone for a walk late in the evening, and had wandered quite far when suddenly the siren on top of the Priory Cinema began to howl. We set course for home at once, and were a few hundred yards from her door when suddenly the air around us was permeated by a peculiar and very unpleasant smell. Assuming instantly and simultaneously that we'd been caught in a gas attack we took off like a pair of greyhounds, burst into her house and snatched up our gas masks. We were about to put them on when we realised that the smell had gone, but we kept them very close to hand throughout an anxious night in her shelter. Only next day, when we mentioned the incident to Tom Rose, did we learn that the smell emanated from the Radiator Works on National Avenue, and was caused by them damping down the furnaces at the sounding of the alert; an operation which generated clouds of foul-smelling steam...

I don't think I've ever felt so stupid.

During this time Albert got some leave and we spent a weekend away at the home of our friends George and Jenny Watson. George had been a colleague at Jacksons, and now worked in the Co-operative Bakery in Coventry. The visit to their city shook us a bit; Coventry had suffered terribly during November 1940, and the extent of the destruction was staggering. Whole areas were in ruins, and I remember we couldn't get close to the remains of the cathedral at all; every route seemed to be blocked by rubble or scaffolding. They told us a bit about the night when it had all happened, and it was pretty horrifying stuff. We thought we knew about air raids but we'd come across nothing like this.

We were heading for it, though, although we didn't realise it. There was nothing dramatic to warn us, just a gradual increase in the intensity of the raids. There was a particularly vicious one at the end of March, with the city centre being hardest hit. One bomb demolished the Metropole Hall on West Street, which was my favourite dance hall. It was a great place; not

(above). The Terrible Trio of No. 6 Fire Force Area, National Fire Service. Left to Right: Meg Smart, Cathy Hunt and myself, pictured in the yard of Central Fire Station on the 26th May 1943.

(right). Firewoman Gladys Petherbridge at work in the control room of the 'White City' Station, Anlaby Road. The control rooms of the various fire stations were virtually identical, and though the main instrument employed was a stick of chalk rather than a computer the mobilisation system worked well despite the intense demands made upon it.

much to look at from the outside, but lovely inside, and for me it had the best dance floor in town. In the days before the war Jackson's used to hold their firm's dances at the Metropole, and it was there that I learned to do the Lambeth Walk. Another bomb destroyed the Alexandra Theatre, on George Street, killing a member of the orchestra there who had been firewatching, another fell close to the Royal Infirmary, then on Prospect Street, blowing out most of the windows, and another almost wiped out a group of Albert's colleagues, blowing apart their trailer pump and its towing vehicle - fortunately after they had dismounted and moved away.

The worst incident, however, was at Shell Mex House, at the junction of Ferensway and Spring Bank, which served as the A.R.P. Control Centre. A landmine came down on the building, blasting it apart and killing a number of people. One of them was Dr David Diamond, the Deputy Medical Officer, who had recently organised a blood donor campaign. In later months we would meet his widow when she came to Central in the course of her welfare work. Another fatality was a young R.A.F. man who was on leave and waiting in the building to take home his fiancé, who was a clerk. And another was P.C. Garton who was on duty at the door. Albert and I had met and become friends with P.C. Garton at a dance at Beverley Road Baths, some months earlier, and whenever we passed the junction we would stop off and chat with him. After the terrible explosion which wrecked the building, no trace of him was ever found except for fragments of his uniform. It took a long time to get used to the idea that we would never see him again.

During April my application to join the Fire Brigade was accepted, and before I knew it I was the proud owner of a uniform, a tin hat and a service gas mask and receiving training in the company of a number of young women of similar age. Of these I particularly remember Vy Grantham, Enid Lacey, Marjorie Reece, Monica Crowther, Cathy Hunt, Meg Smith, Joyce Mason and Irene Callan. Because of the circumstances the training was basic and rather hurried; we had squad drill and lectures on brigade operational structure and the insignia of the various ranks, and who to salute and how. Somehow I never really mastered the art of the salute, and to avoid displaying my incompetence in public I became adept at ducking swiftly into shops whenever I saw a senior officer. We were shown practical things, too, such as how to operate extinguishers and how to tackle incendiary bombs, and we were visited by a Miss Swift who taught us how to use the control room telephones correctly and how to accept and relay the messages which would come to Central Fire Station from Hull Control, which was situated alongside Queens Gardens - even the gardens themselves were geared for war, I remember, with shelters sunk into the middle. Essentially that was deemed sufficient for us to be unleashed on the control room and our unsuspecting officers.

Not that our officers required any protection, having by now adapted to the nature of a wartime brigade in which the seasoned professionals were outnumbered by AFS volunteers with more enthusiasm than expertise. Outstanding among them I remember Mr Paragreen, a bluff, unflappable individual who treated Auxiliaries with a certain wry resignation and had a healthy contempt for any activity other than firefighting. His attitude was superbly demonstrated one day when he detailed a young Auxiliary fireman to wash the kitchen windows. Out of uniform the young man was an accomplished bass player with Tommy Fisher's band - I'd danced to his music at the Newington Dance Hall - but as a window cleaner he proved disastrous. Unable to reach the high window he stood on a boiler, the top of which promptly gave way and dumped him up to his knees in hot water. The ensuing hullabaloo reached the ears of Mr Paragreen, who declined even to enquire who was responsible, simply dismissing the matter with the fatalistic comment: "Don't tell me who's done it - I know. That bugger's only good for playing that big stupid fiddle."

When dealing with the ladies of the control room, however, Mr Paragreen was always courteous, invariably addressing us, en-bloc, as 'You females'. That might not sound too courteous, but there were times during the coming months when he could justifiably have chosen far more scathing terms. Not that we were particularly unruly, we were simply young and high-spirited, and sometimes tempted to bend the more irksome rules. During our initial training exercises, for instance, it was required that we should wear our gas masks at all times. This was a hot and uncomfortable business, but the officer at the other end of the line could tell whether we were wearing them, as they distorted our voices. However, with typical feminine ingenuity we discovered that the same effect could be produced simply by sticking our hankies in our mouths before taking the calls, so this we duly did until Mr Paragreen discovered the trick and bawled us out; courteously, of course.

I recall one major incident which horrified us all during that time, when a land-mine fell on a public shelter on Holderness Road, killing some sixty people. There was something particularly horrible about the mines, the way they drifted silently down on parachutes before going off with a roar that could be heard for miles. On one occasion Albert's crew caught sight of one descending in the distance, and flattened themselves beside their appliance to escape the blast. After the explosion they rose - all except one fireman who lay there writhing. For a terrible moment they thought he had been hit by a splinter, but in fact he was trapped by his head. The detonation of the mine had lifted the whole appliance off the ground, and as it came down it had trapped his helmet. He was released with only his dignity injured.

By May we were familiar with the routine of the control room, and becoming proficient at taking calls rapidly and relaying them to the Mobilising Officer for action. By now it was deemed too dangerous to keep the appliances in their bays at Central, for one direct hit could have put all of them out of action. So immediately a raid was known to be imminent they were dispersed in Kingston Square and the surrounding streets - separate enough for safety but close enough to be mobilised quickly. As well as learning the local mobilisation procedures we soon became familiar with the larger system which was co-ordinated from Regional Headquarters in Leeds, and which enabled us to call upon reinforcements from other areas. I didn't realise how soon it would be before we were relaying such a request - urgently.

CHAPTER FOUR

A CITY IN FLAMES

Every night during that first week of May the bell in our flat gave its double ring, sending Albert racing out to fruitless hours of stand-by duty, waiting for raids that did not materialise. Considering what then happened on the nights of the 7th and 8th I have since wondered whether the Luftwaffe was somehow prevented from finding its target on those preceding occasions, and so finally ended up giving us the entire week's-worth of explosives in two nights!

I remember going on duty on the evening of the 7th, and taking my place at my switchboard in the Control Room. The boards would seem very ancient things now, set beside today's sleek electronic masterpieces. They were made largely of wood - no plastics then - and each resembled a narrow upright piano, but with jack-plugs and sockets instead of keys.

I remember someone passing through Control later and mentioning that there was a 'bomber's moon' in the sky, very full and bright, but we could see nothing of this because the Control Room had no windows, for safety's sake. Just as on the previous nights the sirens wailed, but we soon realised that the alert was justified this time, for we heard the anti-aircraft guns open up. I think it was about midnight when the first explosions came - we felt them as vibrations rather than heard them - and moments later our boards began to buzz.

At first the calls came in a fairly orderly succession, and we wrote down the details carefully on message forms, passed them to Mr Kenningham, the Mobilising Officer, and later heard the peal of the bells as appliances set off for their destinations. Cleveland Street, Montrose Street and Chapman Street were hit in quick succession, and then the explosions could be heard as well as felt and the calls began to multiply relentlessly.

We had an officer called Mr Wood with us that night, and it was his task to maintain a continuous record of the progression of events; calls received, appliances mobilised, incidents attended, and so on. To his credit he laboured valiantly to maintain a coherent picture of the situation, but by about 2.30 a.m. his was becoming an increasingly impossible endeavour. Calls were coming in too fast to be logged, and information on attendances was no longer reliable. With the streets now cratered and blocked by rubble some appliances couldn't reach their destinations, and instead the crews set in to tackle the fires at whatever point they could reach. Even when the location of an appliance was known, there was no telling from minute to minute whether it was still operational - several were destroyed by further bombs or were buried under collapsing buildings. By now we had called for help from outside the city, and one of the reinforcing appliances - a pump from Withernsea - fell victim to the raid almost immediately. It was crushed by a falling building in Chapel Street, and one member of the crew was killed.

Strangely I didn't worry as much about Albert as I had during previous raids, although I was constantly aware that he was out there amidst the chaos that we were charting. I was just so busy that there was no time to think about anything except the job in hand, no time to be anxious about anything except whether we could retain any sort of control over the situation. I'd seen what they'd done to Coventry, and I realised that this was how it must have started for them. Everyone in the Brigade knew how it had ended; the firefighters there had been overwhelmed about four hours into the eleven hour raid, with their Brigade headquarters flattened and their communications system wrecked and their pumps blasted into scrap on the streets. Now it was our turn.

Our boards were jammed with calls and we were no longer writing messages neatly but scribbling frantically. Still the requests for pumps continued to pour in; pumps for Queen Victoria Square, Hessle Road, Anlaby Road, Bond Street, Spring Bank, Park Street, Wright Street, Market Place .... Pumps for the Guildhall, the Corporation bus garage, Ranks Mill, the City Hall, the Royal Infirmary, the Prudential Building on King Edward Street, the Presbyterian Church on Prospect Street, W. H. Smiths big warehouse on Jameson Street, the Seamen's Hostel on Carr Lane .... Pumps for places I'd never heard of and places that were special to me, like Hammonds and Powolny's Restaurant and Riverside Quay.

By now there were no more pumps to send, and whenever one got back it was instantly re-directed to the next job on the board. It felt like they were burning our city down around us, and still we continued to take the calls and record the requests with increasingly desperate calmness. Even as I was scribbling out the interminable stream of message forms I remember thinking "How long can they keep bombing us?" and wondering how long we could hold things together if they didn't stop.

For those in the Control Room it was a strange situation; we were monitoring a disaster yet separated from it. The incoming calls told us of familiar streets burning furiously, of buildings we'd known since childhood being reduced to rubble. We knew that out there in the shrieking night wardens and rescue squads were battling to dig out survivors, and our own firefighters were struggling to contain a hundred conflagrations with insufficient water because the river was low and the mains were smashed. In our window-less control room we could perceive the whole and increasingly horrifying picture, but we were not actually experiencing any of it. We could hear the explosions, and occasionally a near-miss would shake the building, but that was as close as we came to reality that night - while out on the streets people unaware of the big picture were living through personal dramas that would remain vivid for the rest of their lives.

In one of the night's early incidents, for instance, Albert and his crew attended a blazing factory in Cleveland Street, but had no sooner set their pump in when there was an explosion inside the building. Above the roar of the pumps and the crash of falling wreckage Albert heard one of his colleagues shout "Duck!", and duly ducked - at which point a huge refrigerator sailed over his head and landed with a crunch on the pavement beside the pump. Albert never forgot the picture of that big, square, white fridge tumbling end-over-end through the air like a toy kicked by a child.

Later his pump was directed to an incident off Hessle Road. They arrived to find that incendiaries had ignited buildings on both sides of the street, and the towering flames had joined forces in the centre, turning the street into a tunnel of fire. As he described it "Like a country lane with the trees hanging over from each side - but instead of branches and leaves it was a canopy of big golden flames."

My sister Elsie and her two young daughters Annie and Dorrie were at the Holderness Hall Cinema that night, watching Deanne Durbin in Spring Parade. Afterwards they went to a friend's house and later emerged to find that the sky was full of bombers and the moonlit streets had become a battlefield.

The scene that met my eyes after I left Central's control room and made my way to the city centre; a wasteland of smoke-wreathed rubble and gutted buildings. Courtesy Hull City Record Office.

The devastation in the city centre was awesome but amidst it trailer pump crews could be found struggling on, and incredibly they succeeded in bringing all the fires under control. Courtesy Hull City Record Office.

As the bombs crashed down and shrapnel whistled around them they fled for home through the maze of narrow passages between the houses, encountering sheltering knots of frightened people and skirting round wrecked and burning buildings. They made it safely back to their home in Mayville Avenue and spent the night in their shelter, up to their ankles in water and singing 'One Man Went to Mow' to keep their spirits up. Emerging at dawn they found that the raiders had decorated as well as destroyed; one of the night's bombs had exploded in a nearby drain, plastering porridgey mud over every house in the street.

There was another lasting impression that Albert gained that night, and although he was never a religious man it made him an eternal admirer of the Salvation Army. At a time when the only sensible place to be was either deep in a shelter or far outside the city, the Salvation Army were on the surface and in the centre of it all, handing out mugs of tea and sandwiches to the exhausted firefighters. There were other organisations who worked heroically above the ground during the raids; from the Police, wardens and rescue squads to the cycle messengers. But the behaviour of the Salvation Army always struck Albert as particularly impressive because it wasn't their duty to put themselves in harms way, and in bringing comfort onto those dangerous streets they also confirmed the sincerity of their faith in the God they served.

Gradually the ferocity of the raid diminished and the torrent of incoming calls dwindled to a trickle. Over four hundred major fires had been started since midnight, but around 8.30 a.m. we were able to report to Regional Control that all were under control. Only when the next shift came on, at nine, were we able to

venture out and see the reality behind the messages we had been relaying all night.

The devastation was awesome. Acrid smoke was drifting on the air like fog, the streets around Central were littered with debris, and broken glass was everywhere; it lay like a shiny carpet over road and pavement and was piled in glittering mounds in the gutters. It was hard to believe there was so much glass in the entire world. I remember thinking that there must have been thousands of windows around me that I'd never noticed. Now they were no longer in place you couldn't fail to notice them; they crunched like ice under your shoes wherever you walked.

The city centre was a tortured landscape of cratered streets and wrecked buildings, some of them still wrapped in flames. Sections of pavement and roadway had split and lifted as if in an earthquake, and here and there water was gushing up from the broken mains beneath. I passed several crews working jets from trailer pumps, and had to look closely at the faces beneath the grimy helmets because any one of them could have been Albert - exhaustion and soot made them all identical. The roar of the pumps and the crackle of flames drowned out all other sounds, but occasionally there came a grinding crash as some wall or roof collapsed, and then clouds of bright sparks would mushroom up and whirl around on the hot air.

The whole skyline of the city had changed overnight; there were no straight lines or tidy shapes left; every outline was jagged and broken, every building askew. Prospect Street was a line of ruins, with the beautiful church now roofless and smoking. Storey Street and Saville Street were a blazing shambles, the shops reduced to rubble and tangles of

(left). By July 1941 almost every building around Central Fire Station had been hit, and the peacetime tidiness of a well-run station had given way to rubble mounds that even invaded the station yard. Courtesy Hull City Record Office.

(right). By June 1943 order had been restored to the surroundings, but now poor battered Central had become a casualty, losing its roof to incendiary bombs. Courtesy Hull City Record Office.

twisted girders. On King Edward Street the tower of the Prudential Assurance Building still rose defiantly through the fog of smoke and dust like a miniature Big Ben, but it was battered and listing and isolated. Everything else around it had been flattened. Lines of hose snaked across the scene in all directions, and the spray from the jets drifted on the air, mingling with the blowing ash and embers, and the sheets of scorched and charred paper from a hundred wrecked offices. Blast had bent lampposts or decapitated them, and had brought down the trolleybus wires, leaving them draped like cotton across the piles of smouldering rubble.

As I journeyed through this nightmare landscape I met other people like myself, venturing from shelter to view the damage. Having spent the night tucked away in the Control Room I must have looked tidier than most, but I can't have looked any less dazed than they did. Where the heart of the city had been there was only desolation, and the impact of it all was completely numbing. I wanted so much to do something to register my protest at the carnage, but what was there to do? It was so vast it defied reaction. I couldn't even cry.

I worked my way back to New George Street, and eventually Albert returned home looking like a cross between a miller and a black-faced minstrel. He and his crew had spent the latter part of the night at Ranks flour mill, which had been struck by incendiaries. It was so big that once alight it was used as a marker by the bombers, and the firefighting operation had been carried out under a hail of high explosives.

Albert was exhausted and red-eyed from the smoke, his face was spark-burned and he had a groove across his forehead from hours of wearing his helmet. He collapsed into bed after giving only the briefest account of his adventures. Months later, however, a fireman called Jim Wardby remarked to me: "You should have seen your Albert at Ranks. Bombs going off all over the place, and he's working a jet from the middle of the bridge opposite, out in the open and never even ducking when the stuff came down." His words confirmed something that I'd begun to realise; Albert might have been a good sugar boiler in another time, but in firefighting he had found his true vocation. He was small in stature but big in heart, and whenever there was a narrow tunnel to be crawled down or a tiny window to be climbed through, the call would go out for 'Little Albert'.

Albert got little sleep that day because word came that a further raid was expected, and so it was all hands to the station to get hose and other equipment ready. I was off-duty on that second night, but seeing the way things were going it seemed sensible to stay close to Central in case I should be needed, so as night fell I got into uniform again, and when the sirens sounded I walked over and joined the rest of the firemen's wives in the shelter in Central's yard.

The rumble of explosions came almost immediately, the vibration bringing dust sifting down on us from the concrete overhead, and occasionally causing the lights to flicker. There were about thirty of us in the shelter, and everyone was exchanging tales of the previous night's adventures. Periodically we were joined by non-Brigade people who'd been passing Central and decided that discretion was the better part of valour. We welcomed them in and and got news of the latest developments. We heard that the docks were ablaze and that telephone communication was breaking down because some of the exchanges had been hit, and that some of our men had been injured in a building collapse on Anlaby Road. We learned, too, that Ranks flour mill had been hit again, this time by high explosives, and that much of the building and its contents had fallen into the river. I could imagine Albert's reaction when he found out - all the frantic efforts of the previous night had been in vain.

The explosions became louder and more frequent. Suddenly there was a clatter of boots in the shelter entrance, which was L-shaped to shield the occupants from blast, and a dishevelled-looking civilian appeared. From the outside world behind him came bangs and crashes of varying ferocity, but he put his request to us as calmly and courteously as if he were asking permission to shelter from a rainstorm.

'Is it alright if I come in here? It's getting rather bad outside."

I was sitting near the door with Mrs Jowett, the wife of one of our officers. She called out "Of course you can", and we both beckoned to him, but just as he started to move towards us the world went mad. I remember a tremendous bang, and a feeling of great pressure, and instant total blackness as the lights failed. The ground rocked under us, people fell against each other in the darkness and dust and fumes billowed chokingly around us. Somewhere amidst the confusion I realised with stunned amazement that we'd actually been hit. Looking back now that amazement seems almost comical. We'd all been aware for ages that bombs were dropping all around us, but when one actually hit us the immediate reaction was acute astonishment. I suppose that's what enables soldiers to carry on - it's always someone else who's going to be hit, and you never think of yourself as someone else.

There was some shouting in the darkness, but no panic, and after a few moments we were able to assess the situation by torchlight; the dust motes dancing silver in the beam as it played over the jumbled interior. The shelter had taken a hit at the end where Mrs Jowett and I were seated, the blast sealing the entrance and entombing us. At the other end, however, there was an emergency exit walled off with sandbags, and after a few seconds we heard the calls of a rescue squad there, and shouted back to confirm that we were safe. One by one the sandbags were hauled away, releasing a flickering brightness into the interior. I glimpsed a helmet with 'RESCUE' painted on it in neat, white lettering, and saw hands reaching in from the outside to help the first of us out. It was an orderly evacuation, if a bit confused because of the gloom and the continuing din filtering in from outside. Mrs Jowett and I were the last to leave, but just as we reached the door she said: "That man - where did he go?" and I realised that he'd vanished at the moment the bomb struck. We went back together and searched the shelter but there was no sign of him, so we abandoned the quest and allowed the rescue squad to help us out.

Seen from outside, the shelter looked like a boat hit by a squall; battered and listing. But my first thought on emerging was that we were better off huddled in a wrecked shelter than emerging into this shambles. Without the concrete to muffle it the sound of the explosions was deafening, and now, too, we could hear the sinister throb of engines as the bombers passed overhead. Chandelier flares were hanging high in the sky, their brilliance casting a weird, shifting pattern of stark white light and inky shadow over everything. A blizzard of sparks was rising into the air from the direction of Mason Street, the outlines of the station and the adjacent New Theatre were blurred by a haze of smoke, and the yard was littered with debris.

NATIONAL FIRE SERVICE. STATION. A2 X

(right). The personnel of another makeshift fire station; a former garage on Orchad Park. The trophies and prizes were won by one of the firewomen who was an excellent athlete.

(left). It may look quaint by today's standards, but to us the peacetime 'red engines' had a certain glamour that was lacking in the utilitarian grey ones produced for the war. This one is pictured at the 'White City' Fire Station on Anlaby Road.

There seemed to be firemen and rescue workers everywhere, and someone was shouting that one of the appliances had been hit, but I couldn't see where it was and there was no time to look because our rescuers hustled us away from the scene, out into John Street, I think, and round and in through the back entrance of the New Theatre. As we stumbled into the shelter area Mrs Jowett and I discovered that our search had been futile, for standing there was the man whose arrival had preceded the blast. He was covered from head to foot in dust, but astonishingly was unhurt.

If I have one particularly bizarre memory of the Blitz it is of sheltering until the dawn in an elegant theatre, surrounded by a mixture of bedraggled fire brigade wives and actors from the Doyly Carte Opera Company. I remember that the latter kept disappearing from the shelter area on forays to the bar, and that men from Central came in periodically to keep us informed. We learned then that an appliance had in fact been destroyed in the yard, receiving a direct hit just as it was about to move off. The crew of three had been killed instantly. One of them was our friend Bill Hewitt.

Gradually the fury of the raid abated, and at dawn we emerged into the battered, smoke-misted streets, to be met once again by scenes of unimaginable destruction. The city centre seemed to have suffered even more attention than on the first night, or maybe it was just the accumulation of two nights-worth of destruction that made it look so terrible that morning. It was almost impossible to believe that just forty-eight hours earlier this devastated wasteland had been a network of tidy streets flanked by imposing buildings, most of which - like the Presbyterian Church, the Co-operative Store and the Prudential Building - were lifetime landmarks.

Albert had seen the progress of the destruction at first hand. Throughout the night his crew had been fighting fires in the city centre, struggling to contain the separate blazes and prevent them spreading and combining into one massive, all-consuming inferno. His account of one particular episode from that night remains with me to this day. The Royal Infirmary, then located on Prospect Street, had been straddled by incendiaries, and Albert's was one of the pumps dispatched there. One ward was alight when they arrived, but jets were brought into use and the fire was contained and extinguished. Then more incendiaries came down on the building, and Albert and several other firemen climbed up onto the roof and dealt with them in the fastest possible way - by booting them down into the street below. And it was only then that they had chance to take in the scale of the holocaust, for looking out across the city from that height they could see only a sea of fire. Even as he looked out, appalled, Albert saw a stick of bombs come down into the flames, the bright flashes and rumbling detonations throwing up huge billows of sparks.

Albert was a stoical rather than emotional man, and what followed was so uncharacteristic that I had to smile when he recounted it later.

"I was so mad at the sight of it all," he told me, rather sheepishly, "I was so bloody furious I found myself standing up there shaking my fist at the sky, and cursing Hitler for what he was doing to my city."

I smiled at the time, but it is still a picture I treasure in my mind; Albert standing high up on the Infirmary roof, surrounded by fire and smoke, his fist raised in furious defiance. For me it symbolises the spirit of the man, of the Fire Brigade and of the whole city during those two unforgettable nights.

CHAPTER FIVE

INSECTS AND INCENDIARIES

It wasn't until the dust settled and the smoke cleared that we grasped the full extent of the destruction, and realised just how much of the city had been swept away. The scale of the disaster was stunning - in some cases whole streets had been levelled - but the real sorrow came over the loss of individual places. Albert and I had been to a wonderful dinner-dance at Powolny's Restaurant, on King Edward Street, and I'd loved the elegance of the place, and loved the meal. Now Powolny's was no more, just another anonymous ruin in a line of ruins. Even the one place intact on the street, the Prudential Tower, had to be blown up by our own side because it was no longer safe.

Every girl I knew had, at one time or another, treated herself to a hat at Costellos, which stood on the corner of Jameson Street and Saville Street, and now all that remained of it was a gutted shell. The big department stores were gone too; there would be no more browsing around Thornton Varleys, Bladons,

Edwin Davis or Hammonds. The latter's roof-top dance hall had also fallen victim, of course - now it was just a wreck perched high on top of a ruin. Nor would we dance again at the Mecca, with its nice cafe; it was just a twisted mass of debris. Shops, dance halls, cinemas, pubs, restaurants... so many familiar places had vanished so swiftly that as I walked round the city I felt as if my past was being expunged before my eyes.

The expunging continued over the next two months, and the casualties mounted. At Mulgrave Street, near North Bridge, a street shelter took a direct hit and many people were killed. On another night the all-clear sounded in error and a raider dropped several bombs after people had emerged from the shelters, inflicting over twenty casualties. All deaths in war are sad, but that incident struck me as really tragic.

By now my sister Anne had moved out of the city, and was living in Malton, where she worked in a

All that remained of the communal shelter on Mulgrave Street which took a direct hit, killing some 60 people. Courtesy of Hull City Record Office.

37

The wreckage of Spillers, which we assumed was the source of the cricket plague that descended on Central. Courtesy Hull City Record Office

bakery, making sausage rolls and meat pies for the troops. Around mid-July I was granted a week-end leave and went off to visit her. I was due back on duty at 8 a.m. on the Monday morning, but it was so pleasant to be away from the bombing that I stayed over the Sunday night as well, and then scrounged a life back with one of Anne's friends who drove the Danish Bacon Company's lorry into Hull very early on Monday mornings. It was just before 7.30 a.m. when I alighted at the corner of Beverley Road and Spring Bank, and under normal circumstances I would have had ample time to reach Central - but it was soon obvious that circumstances over the weekend had been as abnormal as usual; there were fresh craters all over, and mounds of rubble across the streets, and every diversion took me further from my destination. Since Mr Paragreen was already of the opinion that I was one of the dizzier of his females I didn't want to prove his point by arriving late, so

eventually I broke into a gallop, scaled a few mounds and finally made it into John Street, sweating and dishevelled but with seconds to spare. Then I turned into Worship Street and came to an abrupt halt because I was facing a rope barrier and a very tired-looking policemen, and behind them, directly in front of the station, was the kind of hole in the ground that I had come to recognise as the resting place of an unexploded bomb.

All my galloping had been unneccesary - Central had been evacuated except for the Control Room staff, and nobody on the outside was getting in until the bomb disposal squad arrived and did their job. Accordingly I returned to our flat and recovered from my gallop with the aid of a cup of tea.

Albert was there and looked desperately tired. I'd apparently missed quite a weekend, and he'd spent most of the previous night at Spillers on Cleveland Street, where thousands of tons of grain had burnt. It had been a gruelling battle and a perilous one, with the laden floors of the building collapsing one after the other, and as the water mains around the place had been destroyed they'd had to set up a relay, drawing water from the River Hull and boosting it from pump to pump until it arrived at the fireground.

The fire at Spillers was the biggest of more than eighty that were started that night, and it produced a curious effect - at least we always assumed it was the destruction of the grain that was responsible for the influx that followed. Just as rats desert a sinking ship, so it seemed that insects abandon a burning silo, and over the next few weeks Central was inundated with crickets. They weren't tiny, either, most of them were about two inches long, and in the odd relaxing moment the firemen used to amuse themselves trying to catch them. Around dusk on those summer nights we used to get the cricket chorus, with the creatures whirring away so loudly and persistently that you got the feeling that the station wasn't really surrounded by a battered grey city, but by acres of rolling meadow.

The big problem was keeping that city around us; each night new incident locations appeared on the Brigade's mobilisation boards, from big industrial targets such as Fenner, Reckitts and Sissons down to the little streets that were home to ordinary folks; Cave Street, Da La Pole Avenue, Buckingham Street, Sculcoates Lane, Hall Road, Rokeby Avenue, Willerby Road. Goddard Avenue, Aldborough Grove, Cottingham Road, Summergangs Road, Durham Street, Scarborough Street...the list was endless and every incident meant misery for someone. No night was complete, either, without James Reckitt Avenue getting something. The bombers seemed to have a grudge against James Reckitt Avenue.

Albert was never sure which jobs he hated most; the factory fires were bigger and far more dangerous, but watching people's homes being destroyed was far more distressing. Despite the continuing destruction of the city, and the news of similar raids elsewhere, I don't ever remember anybody suggesting the possibility that the enemy might actually manage to batter us all into submission. The idea that Britain might lose the war simply didn't occur to anyone, and among the firefighters the spirit ranged from grim determination to cheerful optimism. I can only remember one occasion when the atmosphere in the Control Room became tearful; we had the radio on after lunch one day, listening to a 'Forces sweetheart' programme, and suddenly one of our girls - Irene Callan - recognised the voice of her boyfriend, who was overseas somewhere. He told her how much he loved and missed her, and that was it as far as she was concerned - it was tears for the rest of the afternoon!

In August the Auxiliary Fire Service ceased to exist, for all the fire brigades were nationalised into one force, and suddenly Auxiliaries and professionals alike were all part of the National Fire Service. I don't recall that it made all that much difference to us, except Albert was issued with a second uniform and we all had to change our crossed-axes cap badges for the N.F.S. ones. I kept Albert's old crossed-axes badge for a long time, pinned to my handbag, but one day someone unpinned it and took it, which made me very sad.

Around about this time a firewomen's billet was established on John Street, and when things were quiet we were booked off on 'short leave' and allowed to go across there to relax for a little while. Late one evening during that summer I went over there with two other girls for an hour's break, and as all was peaceful we didn't bother to close the blackout curtains, simply shed our shoes and uniform jackets and lay down on our bunks without even turning on the light. About half an hour later, without warning from either the station bells or the sirens, there came a chorus of distant whistling shrieks that terminated in a salvo of heavy explosions. We leapt from our bunks instantly but with the curtains open we didn't dare switch on the lights, and in the gloom we cannoned into each other in ridiculous confusion as we searched frantically for our jackets and shoes. Having finally located them we raced down the stairs and hurtled out into the street; just as a chandelier flare ignited overhead. Suddenly everything was bathed in stark white light, and there we stood paralysed in the middle of the street, like three petrified rabbits caught in the headlights of a car. Somehow we broke the spell and pelted towards Central. Then just as we raced into the yard there was a flash of movement in front of us and above our heads, and for the first time I actually saw the incendiaries arrive instead of just relaying the report of their arrival.

'PLOP!...PLOP!...PLOP!...''

That really was the sound they made as they materialised out of the sky, plonked themselves down in a line across the yard before us and flared instantly into hissing, crackling cauldrons of blue and orange fire. They were so neatly spaced across the concrete that it was uncanny, and the spaces didn't look any too wide. Having screeched to a halt we proceeded to dither; none of us much fancied diving through any of the gaps, which were growing narrower as the flames licked higher and blew around, but neither did we fancy facing Mr Paragreen if we didn't get back to our posts. In the end our fear of Mr Paragreen won the day - we each took a deep breath, sprinted through the nearest gap and eventually erupted into the Control Room just as the first calls began to arrive. Only afterwards did it occur to me that we'd been very lucky indeed; if those incendiaries had been of the explosive type the Brigade would have been short three switchboard operators.

They say that adaptability is the most important characteristic of human beings, and from my experience in those days I'd certainly agree with that. As the weeks passed and summer turned to autumn we came to accept hardships and horrors that once would have been unimaginable, learned to live with exhaustion and snatched meals and shortages, watched with dismay but never despair as our city shuddered under a brutal onslaught that razed its finest buildings and slaughtered its defenceless citizens.

It was in September, I think, that Albert attended his worst job; a communal shelter off Cleveland Street that had taken a direct hit. The occupants had been killed instantly, and the Fire Brigade worked alongside the rescue squads to retrieve their bodies. The memory of that slaughter would remain forever with all those who took part in that recovery operation - I know it did with Albert - but at the time men absorbed the anguish as stoically as their city absorbed its punishment, and like the city they carried doggedly on.

CHAPTER SIX

BATTERED BUT UNBOWED

As the Christmas of 1941 approached the news came through that the Japanese had bombed the American fleet at Pearl Harbour. I remember that during those days we followed the news broadcasts avidly on the radio in the control room, and there was this strange mixed feeling of sorrow and elation. It was as if we'd been struggling desperately while a friend dithered, and now we'd seen them hit by terrible reality, and you didn't know whether to sympathise or say "We told you so!" Overall, though, the feeling was one of mingled relief and optimism. Now there was someone else on our side.

By the end of 1941 I had grown accustomed to my role and was no longer as scared of the officers as I had been in the early days. Without exception they were good men; I particularly remember Mr Denny, Mr Kenningham and Mr Wood - who had been a school teacher - and I could never forget the cool, calm Mr Paragreen. Even the Chief Fire Officer, Mr Barker, was always very amiable and approachable, despite the terrific pressure that he must have been under. Sometimes during the raids he used to stand out on the flat roof above the Fire Force Control Office, scanning with binoculars, looking out for the first glow which was the prelude to a call for Brigade assistance. Around Christmas he complained of the cold up there, and offered a half-pound of butter to the first firewoman who presented him with a balaclava to wear under his helmet. That kind of incentive was too enticing to be ignored; I immediately raked out my knitting needles and within a couple of days he had warm ears and I had a precious half-pound of butter.

During the early evenings, while we waited for the sirens to wail, Mr Kenningham used to send me out for his fish and chips. The fish shop was on Charles Street and I soon came up with a system that enabled me to get a little enjoyment out of the errand. I would dash into the shop and place the order, then race round the block and dive into the Co-operative Hall, on Kingston Square, where dances were regularly held. The atmosphere in there was always wonderful, with the band playing and people laughing and chatting, and the girls waltzing round in the arms of men looking smart and handsome in all sorts of British and allied uniforms. Usually I had just enough time for a couple of dances, then I'd shoot out of the door, run back to the chip shop and arrive back in the Control Room without anyone being any the wiser.

That sort of trick was pretty harmless, of course, but on one occasion my love of dancing led me even further astray and landed me in hot water. It was a curious aspect of the war that despite the horrendous events around us normal Brigade routines were maintained as much as possible, and that meant that standard training had still to be undertaken. Thus it came about that at a time when half the city was in ashes and the Luftwaffe was doing its level best to burn down the other half, we girls were detailed to go across to the sub-station at Blundell's Corner to attend a lecture on...fire prevention!

Needless to say the prospect of a few turns around the floor of the Fulford proved much more attractive than an afternoon spent sitting in a lecture room, so Kathy Hunt and I slipped away from the rest of the party on arrival at the sub-station, and while our colleagues grappled with the triangle of fire and how to forestall it, we demonstrated our mastery of the foxtrot and the valetta. The bepop dance was just coming in but we hadn't got the hang of that yet. All in all we had a great session; and even timed our return impeccably, reappearing just as one of

Central's appliances arrived to collect the party. Unfortunately someone had noted our absence and reported it, and by the following day we'd both received a rocket, and I'd been stopped three days pay. I was as unamused with that as Mr Paragreen was unamused with me. He gave me a ticking-off of his own, ending with the resigned observation: "You always have to go and do daft things. They should call you 'Unorthodox' Baker!"

It was a nick-name that remained with me throughout the rest of my time in the service.

I remember another normal undertaking during that period which had a rather bizarre outcome. This was a Saturday church parade for which we marched all the way from Central to a church in Garden Village, off Holderness Road. A march of that distance was a major test of my co-ordination and the officer's patience because I had this monumental inability to keep in step, but we all arrived there in reasonable order and participated in a service during which the vicar offered prayers for our safety, asking the Lord to look after us and all the other A.R.P. personnel in the days and nights to come. I think we all went away from there a little more uplifted, feeling that we'd gained a bit of divine protection, but then the Luftwaffe spoiled it by coming over the following night and bombing the church flat.

After that it was really left to one of our officers to keep us in good with the Almighty. There was a church on John Street, across from Central, and he used to slip across there whenever he had some spare time, and play the organ. We certainly had a funny bundle of mixed talents.

The raids were no longer as intense as before, but still they were frightening affairs because the scale of the danger for the firemen was not necessarily related to size of the raid. The incident at Saltend had shown that a lucky hit with one high-explosive bomb could create a situation which endangered every crew in attendance, and a hundred jobs since then had shown how a single incendiary could produce a blaze that would, in peacetime, have engaged all the resources of the Brigade. We were dealing with airborne arsonists who carried out their work on a grand scale, and when the sirens announced their arrival each night we could only sit at our boards waiting for the calls to come through and hoping that the bombs would explode harmlessly in the streets, without causing casualties or starting major fires, or that the bomb-aimers might get it wrong by a few seconds and drop their deadly loads into the Humber or on the outskirts where there was plenty of space. Occasionally our hopes were fulfilled; I can remember feeling pleased because they'd flown all the way here just to bomb the grass in some fields near Sutton. So much for the infallible Master Race. Trouble was they got it right more times than they got it wrong, and sometimes they got it more right than others.

I forget the exact night, but it must, have been in the spring or early summer of 1942. It was approaching midnight and the raid had been progressing for perhaps half an hour, with the bombs falling mostly on the East Hull area. I'd already taken several calls through my board, and the number of appliances waiting dutifully in the surrounding streets was gradually dwindling. They were a funny mix, those appliances. Some were the red ones that had protected the city in peacetime, including the Hull Brigade's pride and joy - the huge turntable-ladder that towered up to 150 ft. when fully extended, making it the biggest in the country. The rest were a varied collection; from ungainly-looking battleship-grey tenders hurriedly manufactured for wartime work, down to trailer pumps pulled by taxi cabs. All now bore the National Fire Service insignia, but that was the only visibly uniform element about them. That and the fact that, although kept as clean and smart as possible, all now bore scars of one sort or another; hardly surprising when you think that they were now doing more work in a week than a peacetime fire appliance did in six months, and most of it in very hostile conditions.

I remember completing a message form and handing it over to Mr Kenningham and watching as he entered the details onto his mobilisation board. Then suddenly, without even the usual whistling sound to warn us, there was tremendous crash overhead, and the Control Room shook wildly. All the lights went out immediately, and as I grabbed at my board for support I could feel the building rocking like a boxer who's taken a tremendous punch and is about to fall down. Bits of the place were certainly falling down; through the claustrophobic blackness we could hear crunching, crashing and splintering as bits of wall and roof tumbled down, and I remember thinking "My God, we're going to be buried alive!" And then the rumble of collapsing masonry was joined by another sound; that of water cascading from fractured pipes as the building's plumbing system succumbed to the onslaught of falling bricks. That sound really did frighten me; suddenly we were not just going to be buried alive - we were going to be drowned as well!

The officers were superb in that moment. It would have been so easy to panic, and in the darkness that would have been disastrous. But Mr Paragreen kept control of the situation, and of us girls. As the rumble of falling masonry abated, leaving only the crackle of shorting electrics and the splash of indoor waterfalls, he called out. "Alright, you females, let's have you all out and over to Mason Street".

On Mason Street, almost opposite the 'firemen's pub' - the Old English Gentleman - was a shelter that housed a reserve Control Room, and it was to there that we stumbled, after extricating ourselves from the blackness of poor, battered Central. Within a few minutes we were at our posts in the Mason Street Control Room and back in the war, but I for one couldn't stop shaking for the rest of the night. Within a few days Central was patched up and our Control Room was restored, and it was back to business as usual. But even today, half a century after the event, I can't hear cascading water without remembering that night.

Amidst all the savagery and sorrow there were still lovely moments which demonstrated how the rituals of life still go on, even while there's a battle raging. Mr Barker's daughter Irenee got married, and as she was a Leading Firewoman we girls attended the service as a guard of honour, providing an arch of axes as she emerged with her husband. I had my hair done specially for the occasion; taking my own towel and shampoo to the hairdressers as you had to in those days, with everything in short supply. The reception was held at the City Hotel, opposite the Guildhall, and for that day we simply put away all thought of the war and just enjoyed ourselves like any other wedding party at any other time. We were living through chaotic times, but a girl's wedding day takes precedence over everything.

I remember, too, Albert taking me to the Eureka Cinema on Hessle Road, to see Walt Disney's 'Bambi', which had just come out, and it made me

Irene Barker's wedding, in the middle of the war. Top left is Irene Callan, then Meg Smart and Monica Crowther. Bottom left, next to me, is Vy Grantham – my partner in the great flag-selling project and the fire prevention lecture that never was, at least not where we were anyway.

cry. Strange, I suppose; we were in a war that was making death and destruction commonplace, and I cried buckets because Bambi's mother got shot. I remember us going to the Carlton on Anlaby Road, too, to see Walter Pigeon and Greer Garson in 'Mrs Minever', and loving it so much that we went and saw it a second time.

There were other little diversions too, like giving my friend Marjorie Reece dancing lessons in the Control Room, to the music on the radio, while the switchboards were quiet and Mr Paragreen was temporarily absent. And then there was the flag-selling competition in aid of the Forces, for which the prize on offer for the most successful two-girl team was a fish and chip supper at the Y.P.I., on George Street, as the guests of a group of soldiers. Vy Grantham and I were absolutely determined to secure that prize, and went round the city like a two-girl whirlwind. Instead of simply relying on street selling,

a very uncertain business, we went into factories and offices - from the Hull Brewery on Sylvester Street to the Hull Daily Mail building in Jameson Street, where we were given a tour and shown the presses in operation. Having a couple of uniformed young ladies turn up in their workplace proved an irresistible novelty for most of the men, and sure enough we sold enough flags to qualify for the prize.

The fish and chip supper was excellent, the soldiers were entertaining company and all in all it was a very successful venture. During a raid a few nights later, however, we heard an explosion close by, and a few minutes later Vy Grantham called me from the Control Room for a moment to peer out of the front door that opened into Worship Street. The street was wreathed in smoke and off to the right huge flames were rising from a jagged hole in a block of buildings facing onto George Street. We had enjoyed our last fish and chip supper at Y.P.I.

No more fish & chip suppers... the YPI building on George Street, shortly after our flag day triumph. Courtesy Hull City Record Office.

One morning in the early autumn I emerged from Central after a night of bombing and bumped into one of the firemen's wives making her way home from the shelter. She lived in a flat about Cousins grocery shop in Caroline Street, so we walked home together. When we reached her doorway we could see from the broken windows that her flat had been damaged, and I went in with her in case she needed any help. She did, but it would have taken more than me to provide it. A section of the roof had been blown in, and the interior was wrecked. I remember that quite automatically she picked up a sweeping brush and began sweeping up the glass, dust and lumps of plaster, and I watched her for several seconds before sanity returned and I pointed out the scale of the task was too much. I suggested she return to Central for some more assistance, then I set off towards our flat intending to get some breakfast ready for Albert's return.

There was debris scattered across New George Street; the now familiar jumble of glass shards, splintered tiles and broken brickwork. I didn't realise how familiar it was until I walked into the flat and discovered that most of it had once made up poor old No. 10. At first I thought we had taken a direct hit, but that would have blasted the walls out. As it was the walls were still in place, but very little else. The blast from a near-miss had ripped the roof apart and shattered the interior, smashing furniture and bringing down the ceiling in a huge, cracked 'V' of plaster and broken lats, the point of which was resting on the bed.

Unlike that first time I didn't dissolve into tears. Perhaps I was numbed by the realisation that this time the damage was irretrievable and consequently our days at No. 10 were over. Perhaps it was sheer disbelief at the way a chapter in our lives had come to such an abrupt and brutal end, without either of us even being aware of the moment of its passing.

Albert had been out throughout the night, tackling various incidents, I had sat there in Central taking the calls. At this distance I might even have heard the explosion that took our home away, but I would never know. Mostly, I think, there was simply a feeling of fatalism. It seemed so long ago that I'd been simply a housewife, reduced to weeping by a flat full of oily soot. For too many nights now I had written down messages which described, in the terse, unemotional language of Brigade communications, the destruction of people's homes and beloved possessions. Now I was experiencing the heartbreaking reality which lay behind those messages, and I couldn't cry for myself and Albert without crying for the whole suffering city.

Those who were not present in those days would find it impossible to image the scenes of destruction which the firefighters and rescue teams encountered throughout the residential areas of the city, but these two pictures serve as vivid examples. Courtesy Hull City Record Office.

CHAPTER SEVEN

NEW LIFE FROM THE ASHES

As one door closes another one opens, they say, and so it proved for us. My sister Anne had returned from Malton and was living in a house in Hotham Road, but as she was about to move on once again the place was available if we chose to take it. We chose just that and took it, furnishing it with as much furniture as we could retrieve from the wreckage of No. 10. We never realised at the time that the house we were moving into would remain our home for the rest of our married life, and that there we would bring up two children. That idea would have been far more difficult to credit than the possibility of being bombed out again.

By the end of 1942 Hull had taken a worse hammering and suffered higher casualties than any other city in Britain, in terms of size and losses per head of population. The scale of the city's torment was concealed from the rest of the country, of course by the BBC's use of the description 'a North-East coast town' but as far as the inhabitants were concerned nothing could conceal the extent of this ordeal by fire, or hide the effects. Where once had stood impressive shops and dignified offices there were only expanses of rubble and weeds, while the gutted hulks of factories and warehouses stood crumbling and fire-blackened in the more recently bombed areas, waiting only for the demolition teams to conclude their precarious and perilous existence.

Everybody you met had suffered damage to their homes, from smashed windows to total destruction. Almost everyone knew someone who had been killed or injured; a workmate, and acquaintance, a friend or relative. One raid killed so many that a mass burial was held in Chanterlands Avenue Cemetery.

The whole population seemed to be bonded together by this shared experience, so that kindness and helpfulness were the order of the day, because we were all in the same heavily battered boat in the same raging storm. Never, afterwards, would I experience that same sense of kinship with other people, that feeling of closeness to strangers on the street or in the shops. In a way there were no strangers because we were all sharing the same struggle, and that brought us together. I have sometimes wondered, since, whether the defiant and genuinely cheerful spirit of that time came partly from a heightened feeling of personal esteem. In peacetime it is so easy to feel ignored and unimportant, but nobody can feel insignificant when someone is taking the trouble to send airplanes across to drop bombs on them!

This is hindsight, of course. At the time it was often insignificance that you craved for; the kind that would allow you to disappear into a crack in the pavement. Albert admitted to that feeling without shame. As he said, you could hardly feel more vulnerable than standing upright on the street in the full glare of a fire, unable to move because your hose will run amok if you let go! By now Albert had become a seasoned firefighter, having received what amounted to a two year crash course in major incidents, and early in 1943 he was offered a promotion to Leading Fireman, which he turned down. I felt sad because I believed he would have handled the role well, and would have looked after a crew conscientiously, but his competence was not matched by his confidence, and he was happier as a follower rather than a leader.

By now there was a definite sense that the tide of war was on the turn; the Germans seemed to be losing their grip a bit, and had certainly got themselves into a right old mess in Russia. We assumed that was one of the reasons why the raids became increasingly infrequent. After the end of January came many nights when the Control Room received only requests for attendances at the normal incidents which plague any big city; house fires and small factory blazes and chimney fires at those homes which still had chimneys! But it was impossible to relax; there was still the feeling that the Luftwaffe had not finished with us. Unfortunately some of the population did get a bit complacent and we had trouble with people using the static water tanks as refuse tips, shoving everything from cardboard boxes to old tyres into them - all of which would clog the suction of the pumps and cut off the water supply to the firefighters.

The firefighters themselves weren't always on their best behaviour though. We had a lorry which carried a huge tank of water as a mobile emergency supply, and one warm afternoon a fireman whose home had lost its water supply decided to have a bath in the tank. No sooner was he stripped off and imersed than someone jumped in the cab, drove the lorry out of the yard and did a quick circuit of the city centre, ignoring the bellowed threats from his embarrassed cargo!

I remember June 24th very clearly, for both Albert and I were off duty, and that afternoon we went to the Regal cinema on Ferensway to see 'Random Harvest', with Ronald Coleman and Greer Garson. It was a lovely summer day, and after the show we strolled back to Central hand-in-hand, taking the route down Brook Street, past the ruins of Thornton Varley, and along Albion Street, past the imposing facade of the Municipal Museum; the ground floor of which had been used as a sale room by Thornton Varley ever since they were bombed out. I loved that museum; the contents were fascinating; coins and butterflies and a huge dinosaur skeleton and all sorts of marvellous things, including a great big stuffed Polar Bear that stood in the entrance foyer, eyes and claws gleaming, and looked so real you thought it was going to jump on you. I loved that Polar Bear. I think everybody loved that Polar Bear.

Back at Central we parted. Albert went off to man his appliance but I wasn't due back on duty until the morning. Nevertheless I hung around the station for quite a while, chatting with the girls on duty and wandering out to watch the crews training in the yard and going through the vehicle and equipment checks that are part of a fire station's everyday routine. I remember that my friend Marjorie Reece was one of the girls on the boards that night, and we chatted for ages. It had been a really lovely day and I suppose I didn't want to end it and just wander off to our little empty home. It was nicer to be around with friends. I suppose even I must have become a little complacent by then, or perhaps it had been such a perfect day that nothing could spoil it, but when word of an impending air raid came through I felt almost indignant; how dare they come back and start spoiling everything again!

But dare they did. By midnight I was back in Central's renovated shelter, listening to the familiar drone of bombers, the thunder of distant explosions and the crash of near ones. It was just after a salvo of the latter that someone ran into the shelter - one of the fireman's wives, it was - and told us that Albion Street was ablaze from end to end. Despite the recent close explosions I couldn't credit what she said, so I left the shelter and hurried onto Worship Street, past the front of the Station, with its bays now hollow and empty.

Ablaze from end to end ... The phrase doesn't actually do full justice to the sight that met my eyes as I reached the corner of the building and stared down the street that Albert and I had walked along just a

Goodbye to the beautiful polar bear and hundreds of other irreplaceble artefacts. The Municipal Museum – temporary home for the already bombed out Thornton–Varley – stands gutted, just hours after Albert and I had strolled past on a placid summer evening. Courtesy Hull City Record Office.

few hours earlier. Then it had stretched tranquil in the summer sunlight, now it was a scene straight out of Hell. From Kingston Square to Prospect Street the road was littered with tiles and lumps of masonry. Over it was churning coils of thick smoke, its blackness tinged orange by the columns of writhing fire that now rose in place of the buildings. In the weird, flickering light I could actually see the stone columns that flanked the doorway of the museum, but behind them there was now just an inferno, and though I couldn't cry for our flat I could have wept buckets just then for the beautiful, white, furry Polar Bear that was being destroyed by those flames. We had seen tragedies of all types over the years, and yes, a stuffed animal can't compare with a human life. But the destruction of that lovely creature was not so much a tragedy as an outrage. It was such a beautiful, dignified thing, It should never have been destroyed so wantonly.

By the following morning all that remained of the museum, and most of Albion Street, was a mound of smoking rubble. Those historical artefacts that had survived and could be easily found were retrieved, and the wreckage-strewn site was then bulldozed flat, eventually becoming a car park. Half a century later I would watch as the Phoenix Project excavated the site, searching for the museum's lost treasures, and would remember that night all over again.

The raid of June 24th 1943 is the last that I remember clearly, although I do recall a later raid when they hit the railway bridge on Southcoates Lane, causing it to snap in the middle and collapse. It must have been a night soon after that when a distraught woman arrived panting at Central in search of one of the ambulances that had once been housed there but which had now been moved out to a station of their own. It seemed there was some sort of crisis involving a girl in a house across the road in Mason

Street, and Mr Paragreen detailed two of us girls to nip across and investigate. We went over and discovered that an an ambulance really was rather vital, for in a tiny room, by the light of two candles stuck in a saucer of dripping, a girl was about to give birth. We got the ambulance in double-quick time, and whisked the problem out of our lives, but I remember that incident particularly because it can only have been a short time later that I discovered that I, too, was going to have a baby.

And so my days as a firewoman were numbered, and eventually came to any end. As the months progressed the doctors discovered that my blood pressure was high, and as Hedon Road Maternity Hospital was under strain I was sent off to Gate Burton Hall, a country house at Gainsborough in Lincolnshire. Anne, Mabel and Elsie visited me regularly, Albert got there whenever he wasn't on duty. And eventually, on the fourth day of the fourth month of 1944 I gave birth to a baby girl who weighed four pounds four ounces, and was christened Margaret.

When at last Margaret reached five pounds they allowed me to return home, and it was there, on my first night back in Hull, that I had my final brush with the blitz. Albert had had to go on duty, I was alone in the house, and suddenly I heard the monotonous drone of a V-1 rocket, or a buzz bomb as we'd come to call them. They'd begun arriving before I left for Lincolnshire, so I knew the score; wait until the engine cuts out, close your eyes and count to ten, then open them. If you're still there you've survived. But now I had another life to think about. As the drone of the engine abruptly ceased I scooped up my precious baby and dived headlong into the gas cupboard under the stairs. Seconds later the house shook as the missile came down somewhere on Willerby Road. I stayed in the cupboard for a further hour, cramped and cradling Margaret protectively, but no further attacks ensued.

From that time on my life was taken up more and more by my little girl. In the months that followed I would watch from a distance as historic events unfolded; feel everything from the long agony of Arnhem to the apprehensive elation of the D-Day landings. But for me, as they say, the war was over.

My daughter Margaret at two months old, none the worse for our
undignified dive into the gas cupboard. And the little girl
she was when at last the war was over.

A Victory Parade march-past for the men who saved the city.
At the head is Deputy Chief Officer Frank Jowett, whose wife
was with me in the Central Fire Station shelter when it was hit.
Behind him is Column Officer Harold Paragreen,
the unflappable officer who kept his 'females' in order so well in the control room.

*Firewomen taking part in the Victory Parade. In all some 60 firewomen
had served throughout the blitz, staffing the control rooms on a three shift system,
24–hours a day. My control room dancing partner Marjorie Reece is nearest the camera,
in the second rank. Also present are Vy Grantham, Monica Crowther and
Gladys Petherbridge, who loaned the picture.*

EPILOGUE

When eventually everyone's war was over, and the era of the National Fire Service came to an end, those who had joined as Auxiliaries were offered the chance to become members of the professional Fire Service. Albert accepted that offer, continued to serve with the Kingston upon Hull Fire Brigade and was present at almost every major incident in the years that followed. In 1954 he was awarded the Fire Brigade's Long Service & Good Conduct Medal, but in 1959 his health deteriorated and he was forced to retire on medical grounds. He died in 1978.

Every year, just before Christmas, a fire appliance pulls up outside my home, and a young fireman dismounts and brings to my door a Christmas hamper; a gift from the Fire Brigade Pensions Fund. It is always a very poignant moment for me. The scarlet machine is huge, sleek and streamlined; so different from the ungainly vehicles which, in my day, roared forth from the bays of Central Fire Station to do battle with the Blitz. The fireman bearing my gift is invariably young, fit and smart - identical, in fact, to my late husband and the other men who rode out into the holocaust of a city in flames.

Half a century has passed, and so much in my life has vanished, but one thing I have with me always; the pride I feel at once having served in the company of such gallant men, in defence of the city of my birth.